FEAST DAYS
AND
SABBATHS

1 ARE THEY STILL BINDING?

How many commandments are contained in the Ten Commandments? Does that sound like a foolish question? Then consider the fact that thousands of religious people would give an answer like "94" or "110." You see, there is a strange belief on the part of many that the great God-written law of the Ten Commandments was actually a part of the ceremonial law of Moses which contained scores of specific regulations. They do not see the decalogue as being distinct and totally unique because of its divine authorship. Neither do they see the clear limitation which the Bible sets for this moral code by calling it the TEN Commandments.

It seems quite obvious that one would effectively do away with the "Ten Commandments" by mingling them with ninety or a hundred others and calling them "ordinances" instead of commandments. Such a radical effort has been made to dilute the force of the only words of the Bible which God wrote with His own hand.

Furthermore, the claim has been advanced

that since the Ten Commandments were a part of the mosaic law of ordinances which ended at the cross, we are no more obligated to obey the decalogue than we are to offer lambs in sacrifice.

Is there proof positive in the Scriptures that there was no such blending of the ceremonial and moral law into one? Can it be shown that the Ten Commandments were of a permanent, perpetual nature while the ceremonial law of statutes and ordinances came to an end when Jesus died? Indeed there is abundance of evidence to answer these questions with a resounding yes!

God made known this distinction to His servant Moses, and Moses explained it to the people at Mt. Horeb. "And he declared unto you his covenant, which he *commanded you* to perform, even ten commandments; and he wrote them upon two tables of stone. And the Lord *commanded me* at that time to teach you statutes and judgments, that ye might do them in the land whither ye go over to possess it" (Deuteronomy 4:13, 14).

Please notice how Moses clearly separated the Ten Commandments, which "he commanded you," from the statutes which "he commanded me" to give the people. The big question now is whether those statutes and judgments, which Moses passed on to the people, were designated as a separate and distinct "law."

God answers that important question in such a way that no doubt can remain. "Neither will I make the feet of Israel move any more out of the land which I gave their fathers; only if they will observe to do according to all that *I have commanded* them and according to all the law that my servant *Moses commanded them*" (2 Kings 21:8). Here we are assured that the statutes which Moses gave the people were called a "law." Any child can discern that two different laws are being described. God speaks of the law "I commanded" and also the "law ... Moses commanded." Unless this truth is understood properly, limitless confusion will result.

Daniel was inspired to make the same careful distinction when he prayed for the desolated sanctuary of his scattered nation. "Yea, all Israel have transgressed *thy law*, even by departing, that they might not obey thy voice; therefore the curse is poured upon us, and the oath that is written in the *law of Moses* the servant of God, because we have sinned against him" (Daniel 9:11).

Once more we see "thy law" and "the law of

Moses," and this time the two are recognized as different in content. There are no curses recorded in the Ten Commandments that God wrote, but the law which Moses wrote contained an abundance of such curses and judgments.

The major point of difference between the law of God and the law of Moses, though, lies in the way they were recorded and preserved. We have already cited Moses' statement that God "wrote them (the Ten Commandments) upon two tables of stone" (Deuteronomy 4:13). Compare that with Exodus 31:18, "two tables of testimony, tables of stone, written with the finger of God."

No one can confuse this writing with the way the mosaic law was produced. "And Moses wrote this law ... And it came to pass, when Moses had made an end of writing the words of this law in a book, until they were finished, That Moses commanded the Levites, which bare the ark of the covenant of the Lord, saying, Take this book of the law, and put it in the side of the ark of the covenant of the Lord your God, that it may be there for a witness against thee" (Deuteronomy 31:9, 24-26).

This book of statutes and judgments which Moses wrote in a *book* was placed in a pocket on the side of the ark. In contrast, the law written by God on *tables of stone* was placed *inside* the ark of the covenant. "And thou shalt put *into* the ark the testimony which I shall give thee" (Exodus 25:16).

At this point we can note several distinctions in the two laws. They had different authors, were written on different material, were placed in different locations and had totally different content.

2 THE CEREMONIAL LAW IS AGAINST US

Now let's take a closer look at the ceremonial ordinances that Moses wrote in the book. They were to repose in the "side of the ark ... for a *witness against thee.*" It is interesting to note that the curses and judgments of this law spelled out penalties for transgression which were totally missing from the Ten Commandments. For this reason, the ceremonial law was considered to be a law which was "against" them. Even in the New Testament we read the same descriptive language in reference to that law. "Blotting out the handwriting of ordinances that was *against us*, which was *contrary to us*, and took it out of the way, nailing it to his cross" (Colossians 2:14).

Certainly there was nothing in the Ten-Commandment law that could be defined as "contrary" to Paul and the church to whom he was writing. It was not "against" those early Christians to refrain from adultery, theft, lying, etc. On the other hand, that moral law was a tremendous protection to them and favored every interest in their lives. We have only to read Paul's exalted description of the Ten-Commandment law to recognize that those eternal principles were never blotted out or nailed to the cross. After quoting the tenth commandment of the decalogue in Romans 7:7, Paul wrote these words, "Wherefore the law is holy, and the commandment holy, and just, and good" (verse 12). Then he continued in verse 14, "For we know that the law is spiritual ..."

If the Ten-Commandment law had been blotted out at the cross, would Paul have spoken in such glowing language of its perfection and spirituality? He did not speak of a past law. He said, "the law IS holy ... the law IS spiritual." In other words, it was very much alive and operating when Paul wrote to the Roman church. In contrast he described the handwriting of ordinances in the past tense:

"WAS against us ... WAS contrary to us." It is certain he was not speaking of the same law. One was present and one was past.

Interestingly enough, Paul spoke of the fifth commandment as being in effect when he wrote to the Ephesians. "Children, obey your parents in the Lord: for this is right. Honor thy father and mother; which is the first commandment with promise; That it may be well with thee, and thou mayest live long on the earth" (Ephesians 6:1-3). Again, we find the great apostle affirming that this commandment "IS" not "WAS." Had it been a part of the ordinances described by the same writer in Colossians, he would have said, "... it WAS the first commandment with promise."

In the New Testament Church there was a lot of contention over the subject of circumcision, which was a major requirement of the ceremonial law. In Acts 15:5 we read, "But there rose up certain of the sect of the Pharisees which believed, saying, That it was needful to circumcise them, and to command them to keep the law of Moses."

As all recognize, this could not be referring in any sense to the Ten Commandments. They do not even mention circumcision. Yet Paul declared, "Circumcision is nothing, and uncircumcision is nothing, but the keeping of the commandments of God" (1 Corinthians 7:19). If the law dealing with circumcision was now NOTHING (abolished), then what "commandments" was he exalting as being still binding? One would have to be blind not to see two laws here. The moral law remained, while the law of circumcision (ceremonial law) was abolished.

The truth is that there are numerous references in the Bible which prove that the law of types and shadows, because of its temporary application, was never considered on an equality with the eternal moral law. Its system of sacrifices, human priesthood and feast days were instituted *after* sin entered the world and always pointed forward to the deliverance from sin which would be wrought through the true Lamb and Priest who was to come—Jesus.

The writer of Hebrews spends much time proving that the law of the Levitical priesthood would have to change in order to accommodate the priesthood of Jesus. He did not spring from the tribe of Levi, but from the tribe of Judah. Therefore, we have reference to Jesus "Who is made, not after the law of a *carnal* commandment, but after the power of an endless life" (Hebrews 7:12,16).

This "carnal commandment" dealing with

a human priesthood is found in the handwritten law of Moses. It contrasts sharply with Paul's description of the Ten Commandments as "spiritual" and "holy" and "good." Nothing could be *carnal* and *spiritual* at the same time. Neither could anything be "good" and "not good" at the same time. Yet in Ezekiel we read these words:

"Because they ... had polluted my sabbaths, and their eyes were after their fathers' idols. Wherefore I gave them *also* statutes that were *not good*, and judgments whereby they should not live" (Ezekiel 20:24, 25). Observe carefully how the prophet identifies the Sabbath law, and then immediately says, "I gave them ALSO statutes that were *not good*." Keep in mind that the Ten Commandments were called "holy, and just, and good" (Romans 7:12). Because of its curses and judgments against their continual disobedience, the law of Moses was "against" them and was "not good."

3 THE MORAL LAW EXISTED IN EDEN

The mosaic law is never equated with the eternal moral code which operated from the very beginning of human history. Although they were not written down until Mount Sinai, the Ten Commandments were understood and honored by the earliest patriarchs. Even Cain knew that it was a sin to kill, because God told him that "sin lieth at the door" (Genesis 4:7) after he murdered his brother.

It is impossible for sin to exist where there is no law. The Bible teaches, "for where no law is, there is no transgression" (Romans 4:15). Again we are told, "Whosoever committeth sin transgresseth also the law: for sin is the transgression of the law" (1 John 3:4). This principle is amplified further by Paul's statement that "I had not known sin, but by the law: for I had not known lust, except the law had said, Thou shalt not covet" (Romans 7:7).

These verses nail down the truth that no sin can be imputed where the Ten-Commandment law is not in effect. God's statement to Cain about sin lying at the door was in reference to his plan to kill Abel, a violation of one of those commandments. This is absolute proof that the moral law was in effect at that early date. Later, Joseph revealed that he was aware of the binding claims of that same law. He said to Potiphar's wife, "how then can I do this great wickedness, and *sin* against God?" (Genesis 39:9). He knew adultery was sin.

Abraham was commended by God in these words: "Because that Abraham obeyed my voice, and kept my charge, my commandments, my statutes, and my laws" (Genesis 26:5). It is very obvious that the law which Abraham faithfully obeyed was not the law of Moses, because that law was not given until 430 years later. And we have just established that the Ten Commandments existed before Abraham, condemning even Cain for murder. Neither is it possible for us to conceive that great, godly Abraham was not acquainted with the basic issues of right and wrong contained in the Ten Commandments.

It is absolutely certain that another law was added 430 years later, and it was in addition to the one Abraham kept so diligently. "And this I say, that the covenant, that was confirmed before of God in Christ, the law, which was four hundred and thirty years after, cannot disannul, that it should make the promise of none effect" (Galatians 3:17).

The context of this verse indicates that Paul is talking about the ceremonial law rather than the moral law of the Ten Commandments. In verse ten, he refers to the curses "which are written in the book of the law." We know this had to be the mosaic law because, as we have already noted, there are no curses recorded in the law written on stone.

Can we find further confirmation that this later law was indeed the law of Moses? The answer rests in Galatians 3:19. "Wherefore then serveth the law? It was added because of transgressions till the seed should come to whom the promise was made ..." Here we have two significant facts set forth concerning the law which was added. We are told *why* it was given and also *how long* it would remain in effect. These two bits of information will be considered very carefully since they contain compelling evidence in the case.

FIRST: WHY WAS IT GIVEN? The verse clearly states that it was "added because of transgressions." This is most revealing because we have just established that "where no law is, there is no transgression" (Romans 4:15). One can't be guilty of transgressing a law which does not exist In this case one law obviously did exist; and it had been "transgressed," making it necessary to add another law 430 years after God's covenant with Abraham. And since it is recorded that "Abraham obeyed ... my laws" (Genesis 26:5), we have to believe that that earlier law, which Abraham observed, was the Ten Commandments. Moses had not yet been born, and it could not have been his law.

So what must we conclude from this evidence? The Ten Commandments had been transgressed, making it necessary to add the ceremonial law. Upon reflection, this makes a lot of sense. If a law is made forbidding murder, and it is broken, then another law would have to be enacted to prescribe the penalty or punishment for breaking that first law. We have already established that the Ten Commandments contained no curses (penalties) or judgments (punishments), but the mosaic law was characterized by those very things.

SECOND: HOW LONG DID THIS "ADDED" LAW REMAIN IN EFFECT? The Scripture says, "Till the seed should come." There is no controversy over the identity of that seed. It is Christ. But do we have evidence that the law which was blotted out and nailed to the cross was indeed the law of Moses? Whichever law it was, it is designated as the "handwriting of ordinances." Nowhere are the Ten Commandments identified as ordinances. That term is applied to local legal codes which are very narrow and limited, such as "town ordinances" which extend only to the city limits. In comparison, the Ten Commandments are more like the constitution of the United States.

4 WHAT LAW WAS BLOTTED OUT?

But let's look closer at that text in Colossians 2:14-16 to get the real picture. After describing the "blotting out" and "nailing" of the ordinances, Paul wrote, "Let no man THEREFORE judge you in meat, or in drink." The word "therefore" means "based on what has just been said, we must come to this conclusion." In other words, he was saying, "Based upon the fact that the ordinances have been blotted out, THEREFORE let no one judge you in meat or drink."

Now we begin to see clearly which law was under discussion. Is there anything in the Ten Commandments about meat and drink?

But let us read the rest of the text before us:

"Let no man therefore judge you in meat, or in drink, or in respect of an holyday, or of the new moon, or of the sabbath days: Which are a *shadow of things to come*; but the body is of Christ" (Colossians 2:16, 17).

Question: Could these sabbath days be talking about the Seventh-day Sabbath of the ten-commandment law? No. Because they are clearly defined as "shadows of things to come." Please keep in mind that the weekly Sabbath was instituted by God before sin came into the world. THERE COULD NEVER BE TYPES OR SHADOWS BEFORE SIN EXISTED! All the shadows were introduced *because* of sin and pointed forward to the deliverance from sin through Christ. For example, all the lambs slain represented Jesus, the true LAMB, who would die for the sins of the world. If sin had not entered the world, there would have been no need of a Saviour, and therefore, no lambs or shadows pointing to a Saviour.

So these "sabbath days which are a shadow" could not possibly be referring to the Seventh-day Sabbath. But what other sabbaths could they be talking about? Were there "sabbaths" other than the weekly Sabbaths? Yes, there were yearly sabbaths which had absolutely nothing to do with the Seventh-day Sabbath of the decalogue. And they were definitely a part of the "ordinance" system which ended at the cross.

For proof of this, let us go back to the law of Moses and read about these annual feast days which were shadowy sabbaths. "Speak unto the children of Israel, saying, In the seventh month, in the first day of the month, shall ye have a sabbath, a memorial of blowing of trumpets, an holy convocation" (Leviticus 23:24). Again we read, "Also on the tenth day of this seventh month there shall be a day of atonement ... It shall be unto you a sabbath of rest" (verses 27, 32).

As you can clearly see, these annual sabbaths fell on a different day of the week every year, and God specifically explained that they were not to be confused with the weekly Sabbath. "These are the feasts of the Lord, which ye shall proclaim to be holy convocations, to offer an offering made by fire unto the Lord, a burnt offering, and a meat offering, a sacrifice, and drink offerings, everything upon his day: BESIDE THE SABBATHS OF THE LORD" (verses 37, 38).

Now we can understand what Paul was referring to in Colossians when he wrote about meat and drink and sabbath days which are shadows. There were certain prescribed offerings for each of those yearly feast days, and they were shadows pointing to the future sacrifice of Jesus. But the Bible says these were "BESIDE THE SABBATHS OF THE LORD," or the Seventh-day Sabbath.

Now it is fully established which law was blotted out and nailed to the cross. At the moment of Christ's death, the veil of the temple was ripped from top to bottom by an unseen hand (Matthew 27:51). The most holy place of the sanctuary was exposed where the sprinkled blood recorded all the sins of the people. But no more blood needed to be sprinkled; no more lambs needed to be slain; the true Lamb had come to which all those sacrifices pointed. From henceforth, it would be a denial of the Saviour to bring animals. It would be denying that He was the fulfillment of all the shadows and types. Therefore, it would be "against us" or "contrary to us" to continue observing that mosaic law.

To clarify this issue further, let's ask a very simple question or two. On the day before Jesus died, would it have been a sin for a man to refuse to bring a lamb in order to have his sins forgiven? The answer, of course, is yes. It would have been a sin, because that was the only way to be forgiven. Another question: Would it have been a sin to refuse to bring that lamb, THE DAY AFTER JESUS DIED? No, because the true Lamb had died, the veil had been rent, and the ordinances blotted out. A law had been abolished by being nailed to the cross—the ceremonial law of Moses. Paul referred to the same law in Ephesians 2:15, "Having abolished in his flesh the enmity, even the law of commandments contained in ordinances ..."

Now let's ask another question: On the day before Jesus died, was it a sin to steal? Undoubtedly it was. On the day after He died, was it a sin to steal? The answer is yes; it was just as wrong as the day before He died. Obviously, all the blotting out of ordinances, types and shadows did not affect the great moral code of the Ten Commandments in the slightest degree—they all applied afterward as much as before Christ died.

There are Christians today who still insist that the yearly sabbaths should be observed along with the weekly Sabbath. If such is required, then what were the sabbath days which were blotted out and nailed to the cross? And what was the "holyday" mentioned by Paul as being abolished along with those "sabbath days which were shadows of things to come?"

The Greek word for "holyday" is *heorte*, which is also used to designate one of the yearly festivals of the Jews: "After this there was a feast (heorte) of the Jews; and Jesus went up to Jerusalem" John 5:1. This is unquestionably one of the holy days that Paul spoke of as being abolished. In contrast, the weekly Sabbath is never referred to as a "feast," neither is it ever connected to the Jews by such terms as "sabbath of the Jews." It is only designated as the "sabbath of the Lord."

It is of more than passing interest that some of the most noted Bible commentators (including Adam Clarke and Albert Barnes) agree that Paul is not talking about the Ten Commandments being abolished at the cross. Dwight L. Moody, Dr. C. I. Schofield and Billy Graham also strongly affirm that the law abolished was the ceremonial law.

5 THE TEN COMMANDMENTS IN HEAVEN

Perhaps we should ask right at this point, what is the significance of the tables of God's law being placed inside the ark of the covenant?

Remember that this spot was the most holy on the earth because it represented God's throne. God had said, "there I will meet with thee, and I will commune with thee from above the mercy seat, from between the cherubims" (Exodus 25:22). Below that shekinah glory, symbolizing the presence of God, lay that holy law by which sin was to be defined. And there, as we know from the Scriptures, Jesus, our High Priest, was to plead His blood for sinners.

The earthly sanctuary was copied by Moses from the pattern in heaven. All its priestly ministry was a type and shadow of the work of Jesus, the true High Priest, in the holy and most holy places of the heavenly sanctuary. "Christ is not entered into the holy places made with hands, which are the figures of the true; but into heaven itself, now to appear in the presence of God for us" (Hebrews 9:24). John the Revelator beheld the original sanctuary in heaven where Christ now ministers as High Priest to make atonement for sin. What is sin? "Sin is the transgression of the law" (1 John 3:4). Which law? John gives the answer in Revelation 11:19, "... the temple of God was opened in heaven, and there was seen in his temple *the ark of his testament*."

Think of it for a moment! This is the real

thing from which all the Old Testament was patterned. Here is the real Priest, the real mediation, and IN THE ARK OF THE COVENANT, the real Ten Commandments. But please consider this horrendous scenario— IF THE LAW THAT WAS IN THE ARK WAS ABROGATED AT THE CROSS, CHRIST IS MEDIATING FOR THE TRANSGRESSION OF AN OBSOLETE LAW! Keep in mind that John is beholding this heavenly scene years and years after the cross. It is still there today! In the throne room of God, over the mercy seat, where His blood is now sprinkled for the blotting out of sin. Sin is still what it has ever been, and Christ ministers His blood for sin. No wonder the mercy seat is located just above the broken law. Remove the ark containing God's law and you remove the foundation of His throne, His government. You also remove the law by which sin can be defined and judged. If there be no law, there can be no transgression, and therefore, no need of an Intercessor or a Saviour.

With the heavenly sanctuary located so definitely in the throne room of God over the ark containing the Ten Commandments, there is not a shred of evidence remaining against the validity of that law. The truth is that all men will be judged on the basis of that eternal code which forms the foundation of God's government. James wrote, "For whosoever shall keep the whole law and yet offend in one point, he is guilty of all. For he that said, Do not commit adultery, said also, Do not kill. Now if thou commit no adultery, yet if thou kill, thou art become a transgressor of the law. So speak ye, and so do, as they that shall be judged *by the law of liberty*" (James 2:10-12).

Do not by any means miss the tremendous truths contained in these verses. This is the law we will be judged by! Which law is it? James leaves no room for doubt. He quotes two of the Ten Commandments. But notice how he defines this law as a complete unit in itself. He states that we are responsible for keeping "the whole law." How many commandments are contained in "the whole law"? Exactly ten! What do we become if we break any one of the ten? "A transgressor of the law," James answers. And that is what sin is called in the Bible. "Sin is the transgression of the law" (1 John 3:4).

Why did Jesus come? "Thou shalt call his name JESUS: for he shall save his people from their sins" (Matthew 1:21). Notice that Jesus came to save us *from* breaking the law, but "... *if* any man sin, we have an advocate with the

Father, Jesus Christ the righteous" (1 John 2:1). Here we have a picture of our High Priest, our Advocate, interceding with His own blood in the heavenly sanctuary before the Father's throne in behalf of those who break His law. Where is the throne located? Over the ark of the covenant containing the law by which James says all "shall be judged."

Is there any validity to the argument that the Ten Commandments were all abolished at the cross, and then nine of them restored in the New Testament? This is a specious invention to attempt evasion of the fourth commandment. No Christian has ever found fault with nine of the commandments. Why would they want to get rid of the fourth? Obviously because they are breaking it and do not want to believe that they stand condemned by it. Can they annul the entire decalogue, and then reinstate nine of them? We have proven already that only the mosaic law was annulled—not the Ten Commandments. Further, James has declared that the *whole* of that law is binding, and breaking any one of them is sin. How can anybody extract the fourth commandment from the Ten Commandments and still call it a "whole law"?

Incidentally, the Sabbath is mentioned in

the New Testament more than any of the other nine. This could be tied to the fact that God has apparently chosen the fourth commandment to be the great test issue in His law. In Exodus 16 He used the Seventh-day Sabbath to "prove them, whether they will walk in my law, or no" (Exodus 16:4).

Is there reason to believe that the Sabbath contains a testing quality that cannot be found in any of the other nine commandments? It is an interesting question to contemplate. Besides being worded in a totally different manner ("remember" instead of "thou shalt not"), the fourth commandment is the one which does not have a stigma attached to breaking it. One might abstain from stealing for fear of going to jail, and from adultery for fear of getting shot by an angry spouse. In fact, it is illegal to break some of the Ten Commandments, so they might be obeyed simply to avoid the negative consequences of disobedience. BUT CONSIDER THIS: IN OUR WORLD TODAY, THE FOURTH COMMANDMENT ACTUALLY CARRIES A STIGMA FOR KEEPING IT! In fact, the only reason one would choose to obey it is out of love for Christ and choosing His will above our own. Therefore, it would constitute a special test of genuine love for Christ.

6 PROOF THAT THE SABBATH REMAINS

Although there is a wealth of proof that the Ten-Commandment law and the Sabbath were confirmed by an obedient New Testament Church, I would like to focus on one area of evidence that is often overlooked or misinterpreted. We find it in Hebrews 4, and it probably constitutes the most convincing single reference in favor of Sabbath-keeping to be found in the Bible.

As a little background, we need to examine the thrust of the whole book of Hebrews. The writer of this letter is showing how many of the elements of the old covenant have been taken away. We can almost feel the anguish of the Hebrew believers as Paul explains to them how the sacrificial system has been taken away, having been fulfilled in Christ. The Levitical priesthood has been removed, being replaced by Christ our High Priest. Were they waiting fearfully to hear him take away the Sabbath also? If so, they must have been tremendously relieved when he wrote these words, "There *remaineth* therefore a 'keeping of the sabbath' (see margin) to the people of God" (Hebrews 4:9). I am using the marginal reading of the *King James Version* because that is the exact, literal meaning of the original statement.

The context of Hebrews three and four does not indicate that Paul was trying to convince the Hebrew Christians which day to keep holy. They already knew that. His great burden was for them to enter into a spiritual relationship with Christ—to have an experience of rest from the works of sin. He proved that the children of Israel did not find that true rest because of their lack of faith and disobedience in the wilderness. Although the Greek word for rest, KATAPAU-SIS, means simply "cessation from work," the context seems to indicate that the author is talking primarily about finding a spiritual rest in their experience.

Nevertheless, the two chapters definitely tie the spiritual rest to the Seventh-day Sabbath-keeping initiated and commanded by God in the beginning. Otherwise, we would not find in verse four a direct quote from Genesis 2:2. "For he spake in a certain place of the seventh day on this wise, And God did rest the seventh day from all his works" (Hebrews 4:4).

The reason for citing God's resting on the Sabbath from His work of creation is revealed only when we analyze verses nine and ten. Paul says that what remains for God's people is not KATAPAUSIS (a spiritual rest), but SAB-BATISMAS, meaning a literal keeping of the Sabbath. Then in verse ten we find the real key which proves beyond a question that the SAB-BATISMAS rest was not spiritual only, but a cessation from physical work. "For he that is entered into his rest (KATAPAUSIS—spiritual rest), he ALSO (in addition to the spiritual rest) hath ceased from his own works, AS GOD DID FROM HIS."

The big question about this verse focuses on the works which one ceases from. Are they works of sin? Are they works to obtain salvation? Or are they the physical works from which we cease on the Sabbath? The answer is plainly revealed by the phrase "AS GOD DID FROM HIS." Go back to verse four and we begin to understand why this quote from Genesis is included in Paul's discourse. It is necessary to establish which works God did rest from. God ceased from His physical work of creation on the seventh day, and we are admonished to cease from ours, as He did from His. He did not just enter into a spiritual rest on the seventh day or we might conclude that He was not at spiritual rest on the first six days. The fact is that God is always at spiritual rest.

Neither did He have any works of sin or the flesh to cease from. He simply rested on the seventh day from His work of creation, and we are being told by Paul that the ones who truly have received the spiritual rest of salvation will ALSO cease from their physical works on the Sabbath, AS GOD DID FROM HIS.

Don't you see how this lends a tremendous new spiritual dimension to the keeping of the Sabbath? It memorializes our personal salvation experience. It stands as a blessed weekly reminder of the continual rest from sin that we may have through Christ. No wonder the Sabbath "remains" for the people of God! Our Creator has made it a symbol of the sweetest spiritual blessings available to the human family.

We can understand why God did this when we pause to think how Sabbath-keeping parallels the salvation experience. What really makes something holy? In Isaiah 58:13 God calls the Sabbath "my holy day" and "a delight." Listen! It is the presence of God in something which makes it holy. (Remember the burning bush?) God's presence is in the Sabbath just as His presence is also manifest in the life of a genuine Christian. So why should not true Sabbath-keeping be made a memorial of true salvation in Christ?

It is no happenstance that the same Hebrew word, CHASID, is used in Isaiah 58:13 to describe the Sabbath ("my HOLY day") and also in Leviticus 19:2 to describe God's people ("Ye shall be HOLY"). He dwells in the Sabbath, and He dwells in His people as a sanctifying influence, hence both are called "holy." This is why God made the Sabbath, from the beginning, a sign of sanctification. "Moreover also I gave them my sabbaths, to be a sign between me and them, that they might know that I am the Lord that *sanctify* them" (Ezekiel 20:12). *The New International Version* says, "so they would know that I the Lord made them holy."

Lest someone raise the stale argument that the Sabbath is only a sign of holiness for the Jews, let me hasten to add this inspired text: "if ye be Christ's, then are ye Abraham's seed, and heirs according to the promise" (Galatians 3:29). All born-again Christians are the true Israel today, and have been sanctified unto God. therefore, the Sabbath is for them.

This sign of sanctification has been reaffirmed in the New Testament by Paul's dramatic statement in Hebrews 4:9, 10 that the keeping of the Sabbath remains for God's people. Because we have entered into His spiritual rest of salvation ("Be ye holy"), he declares that we should ALSO rest from our works, "AS GOD DID FROM HIS" ("my holy day").

Someone might suggest that after we enter into spiritual rest there would be no need to observe the memorial of it by keeping the Sabbath physically. But if that were true, we would have to also stop practicing water baptism. Immersion memorializes our death to the old man of sin. We experience that conversion BEFORE entering the water to be baptized. If the physical observance is unnecessary just because we have had the spiritual symbolism fulfilled in us, then we should abandon the physical custom.

Further, we would have to renounce the practice of celebrating the Lord's Supper. It also memorializes an experience of the heart in receiving the sacrifice of our Lord by faith. But should we give up the physical observance of the communion just because we have already entered into the spiritual joy of what it represents? Of course not! Then why should anyone suggest that the Sabbath not be observed physically just because it is used as a memorial of union with Christ? Paul says that it REMAINS as a Sabbath rest for the people of God.

In their monumental *Commentary On the Whole Bible*, Jamieson, Fausset and Brown make this comment on Hebrews 4:9, "This verse indirectly establishes the obligation of the Sabbath still" (page 449). It is most interesting that these Sunday-keeping theological scholars, with the highest of linguistic credentials, make such a statement. Yet the relationship of the spiritual rest of salvation and the physical Sabbathkeeping is undeniable in the context.

So how can we summarize our discoveries about the two laws? Surely it has been established that the Ten Commandments were in a different category than the temporary mosaic law of ordinances. That moral code, encased in the ark of testimony, like the rest of the wilderness sanctuary, was a copy of the true pattern in heaven. So we affirm that it not only was repeated and reinforced in the New Testament but was identified in John's vision beneath the mercy seat in the heavenly sanctuary, from which Christ ministers His own blood for the transgression of that holy law. From that foundational position, it continues to be the basis for Christ's intercessory ministry for us in the throne room of heaven. Therefore, it is established as the most unmovable and unchangeable of all God's decrees.